Facts About
MAGNETS

by Anita Holmes

HOUGHTON MIFFLIN   BOSTON

A magnet can help you pick something up without touching it.

Magnets are great. Magnets can make some things move without touching them. They can attract or pull some things toward them. They can repel or push some things away.

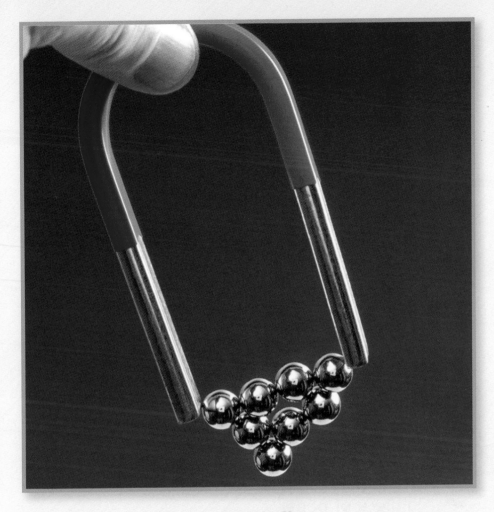

A magnet can pick up steel balls.

Magnets don't attract all materials. They attract only some kinds of metals. They attract iron and steel.

A magnet can pick up things through a piece of paper

Magnets can work through certain kinds of materials. You can cover a magnet with paper and it will still work. Magnets can also work through glass and water.

A magnet may be shaped like a circle, a horseshoe, or a bar.

Magnets come in many shapes and sizes. Some are stronger than others. Strong magnets can move or attract more things than weak magnets. They can move or attract heavier things.

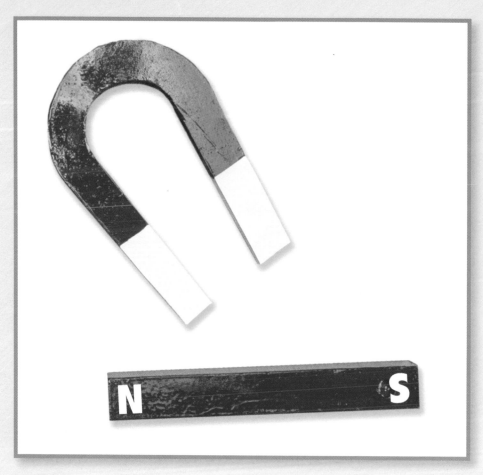

Find the north and south poles on the bar magnet.

The strongest parts of a magnet are called poles. All magnets have a pole at each end. One pole is called the north pole. The other pole is called the south pole.

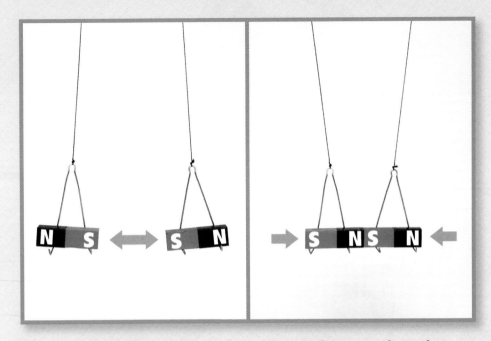

The first picture shows that like poles repel each other. The second picture shows that unlike poles attract each other.

The like poles of two magnets repel each other, or push away from each other. The unlike poles attract each other, or pull toward each other. Suppose you point the south pole of one magnet at the south pole of another. They will push apart. If you point the south pole of a magnet at the north pole of another, they will pull together.

A strong magnet can even pick up cars.

There are many uses for magnets. They can be used to pick up things. They can be used to hold things. They can be used to move things.

Can you think of other ways to use magnets?